DEATH

The Epithet of Excellence

For permissions, workshops, or communal use inquiries, contact:
https://linktr.ee/franklyn3i

First edition

Paperback ISBN: 979-8-9987699-0-0
Hardcover ISBN: 979-8-9987699-2-4
Ebook ISBN: 979-8-9987699-3-1

DEATH

The Epithet of Excellence

Franklyn James

Contents

"A good poem closes like a door left open."

Author's Notes

This poem is an elegy, yes, but not to one person and not to one death.

It is an invocation of Death as a presence, artist, architect, and memory-maker. The voices in this litany: comedians, visionaries, mystics, and martyrs, are all masks Death might take on. Each stanza is a door into grief, but also into imagination, ritual, and cultural memory.

The name *Aphadonis* is not random. It is a merging of Aphrodite and Adonis, symbolizing love, tragedy, guilt, shame, and death. Aphadonis is myth and muse, lover and symbol. And yes, Aphadonis is also Death.

Aphadonis came from a longing to name someone I once loved.

Not to label them but to give shape to something I could never fully explain. Someone whose beauty, compassion, and courage remain unmatched in my memory.

In that way, this poem is personal.

But it does not end with me.

It waits for the names you carry.

All pronouns that refer to Death, such as You, Who, and Her, are capitalized throughout as part of this work's theological and poetic voice.

Preface

Death: The Epithet of Excellence began before I knew it would be an assignment and then a personal engagement, a mission, a calling. It started as a series of poetic meditations, grief given language, love given form. Later, when I learned that an original poem was required for my course in Pastoral Psychology: Dying, Death, and Bereavement, I returned to these words and shaped them into something more: a liturgy of names, an altar of grief, a theology in motion.

This resource is a work of poetry, theology, and cultural reflection. Drawing on public figures and artistic legacies, it reimagines Death as a composite of artistry, memory, lament, and sacred imagination.

Rather than defining Death as singular or final, this work reframes Death through memory, beauty, rupture, resistance, and myth. Here, Death is not faceless. Death is not silence. Death is a maker. Death is named.

Each section explores a different role or domain: art, sound, lament, comedy, and justice. Through these, the poem names Death by honoring those who have shaped how we live, laugh, mourn, and remember. It invites the reader not to fear Death but to speak with it, listen, reflect, and participate.

This piece of work is both a poem and a practice.

How to Use This Book

This book serves as a poetic resource. A work to be read, heard, held, and responded to. It can be used in solitude, a circle, or a sacred space.

The book is divided into two main parts:

1. Part I: Meet Death. A full, uninterrupted reading of *Death: The Epithet of Excellence*, accompanied by curated images. This section is designed to be experienced contemplatively, with each stanza given space to breathe and each image to deepen the moment.

2. Part II: Companion Resource. A collection of prompts, rituals, and group facilitation notes corresponding to each section of the poem. The companion resource offers guidance for spiritual retreats, workshops, community rituals, or personal journaling.

For Individual Use

a. Read the poem straight through first, allowing the visuals and language to wash over you without analysis.

b. Revisit individual stanzas slowly, reflecting on the imagery or reading them aloud.

c. Use the Companion Resource to journal, meditate, or write your own additions to the litany.

For Group or Retreat Use

    a. Begin with the poem as a live reading, projected text, or private encounter

    b. Use the Companion Resource as your guide for conversation, ritual, or writing practice.

    c. Invite participants to respond with stanzas of their own, names they carry, or images of Death they have known.

Whether you arrive as a mourner, an artist, a spiritual leader, or a seeker, this work meets you where you are now. It is not meant to be finished, it is meant to open.

However you enter, may this book offer you breath, witness, and a door left open.

Part

I

Meet Death

I. *Prologue: Naming My Guest*

Oh, this beautiful thing called Death.
How can one fear such a friend?
Some name Death: He, She, or It.
As my guest, Death arrived as Aphadonis.

II. *The Artists of Loss*

Death! The Michelangelo of Mourning,
chiseling grief from hardened souls.
As the Picasso of Pain,
He brushes sorrow toward its goal.

Ye, Shakespeare of Shards and solemn sonnets,
scripting fate when no voice commands.
Da Vinci of Darkness, shaper of Dusk,
You sketched the night with borrowed hands.

The Pietà by Michelangelo

III. *The Sound of Departure*

You, Rachmaninoff of Reveries,
Whose melodies rise, then wane.
Like Proust at the edge of partings,
You captured lost time in chains.

Melancholy by Edgar Degas.

O Pärt of Pause, where sadness plays,
each note a plea, each chord a fright.
Kubrick of Closure, wide-eyed dusk,
You cut life's reel with joyless delight.

The Starry Night by Vincent van Gogh

IV. *Vision and Dream*

Behold the Van Gogh of Vanishing
Your swirls cast dying stars in grotesque arrays.
O Ruthless Rodin of Repose,
sculpting stillness in the days.

Gaze upon Death, the Warhol of Weeping,
looping memories in endless repeat.
As the Dalí of Desolation,
You paint where dreams bleed and meet.

The Incredulity of Saint Thomas by Caravaggio

Come, O Matisse of Magical Moments,
moving through remnants of the past.
The Monet of Melancholic Moods,
Who brushes hues that only time outlasts.

As the Escher of Enigmas,
You conjured labyrinths where meanings blur.
The Caravaggio of Contemplation
revealing dramas sacred and obscure.

V. *The Writers of Grief*

Are You the Hemingway of Heartache,
crafting tales that leave us raw?
Or the Dickens of Departures,
writing sorrow into law?

He's coming, the Tolstoy of Twilight's End,
meditating on the soul's pending plight.
Aha! 'Tis the Twain of Transitions,
twisting fate with wry delight.

Old Man in Sorrow by Vincent van Gogh

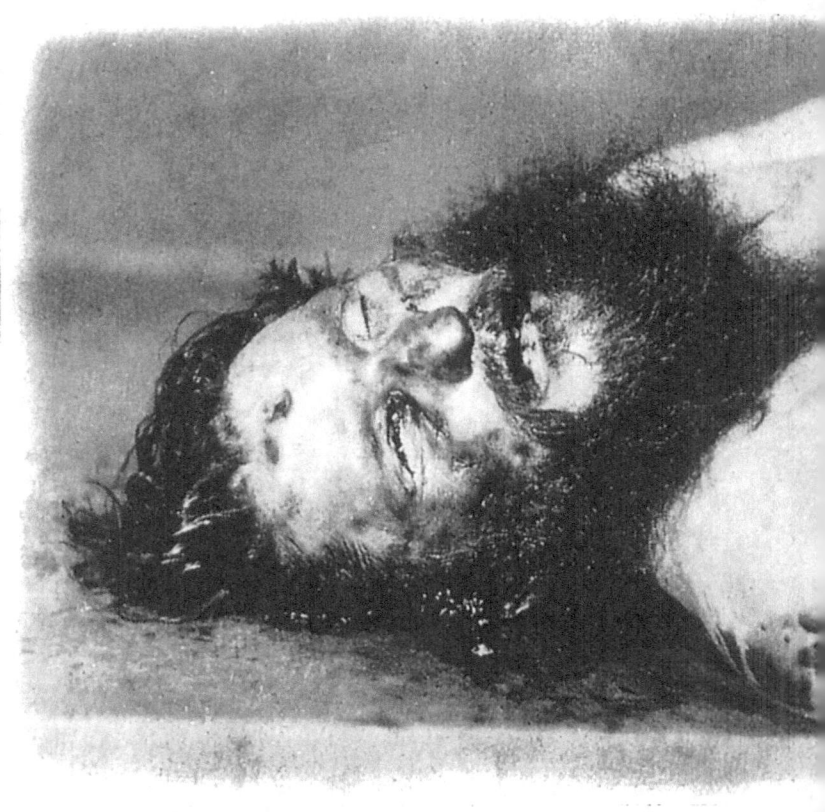

VI. *The Comedy and Chaos of Dying*

Lo, Lucille of Laugh, Levity, and Legacy,
beckoning tears like a midday rom-com.
O Chaplin of the Charnel Chapel,
You usher the Reaper to a scheduled sitcom.

Death, the Radner of Ravenous Ruin,
stitching the woes with the weal.
As the Carlin of Caustic Comedy,
You make the fit slip on Mortality's banana peel.

All Rise, the Magnificent Millican of Mirth,
brewing endings into bitter rebellion.
O Williams of Wit, Wild, and Wired,
stand-up prophet of fractured connection.

Bonaparte of Blood-Bound Borders,
crowned with fire, You carved maps with fear.
O Rasputin of Refuge and Reverie,
You braided hope from foul despair.

Post-mortem photograph of Grigori Rasputin, 1916.

VII. Lament and Mystery

It's Orpheus, orating omens for the grievers,
eliciting dirge even the gods could not avert.
Hildegard of Holy Hum and Herbal Hymn,
You healed the hush between heaven and hurt.

Nightingale of Nature and Nurture,
tending the wounds that have no name.
The Lovelace of Loops and Languages,
lacing longing into ledgers of pain.

Daughters of Sorrow (Luke 23:27–28)

Yes! You are the Pollock of Passing,
splattering fate in chaotic waves.
The Brontë of Burial,
brooding over lichen-clad graves.

O'Keeffe of Openings, the oscillating scythe,
You cut the bloom before life is sown.
As the Kusama of Cosmos,
You scatter ghosts across the timeless zone.

The Raven: *It leaves but half an elusive cry fading into wind.*

Death, the Bourgeois of Buried Bloodlines,
Your spindled shapes recall the pain.
As the Hadid of Horizon's Hinge,
You frame farewell in future planes.

Mark His form, the Gehry of Grief,
crafting bold curves where echoes weave.
The Sartre of Sighs and Sacrifice,
probing why the mourners grieve.

VIII. *Song, Spirit, and Reckoning*

Alas, You Seuss of Soul's Surrender,
You rhymed the end with ticking clocks.
The Hendrix of Illusion, Harlequin's Hostess,
You care not for names nor trades when You knock.

The Court of Death by Rembrandt Peale

Hear ye, the Braxton of Broken Benedictions,
You evoke ballads where love cannot stay.
Mark but this, O Enya of Enchanting Elegy,
Your chants haunt the halls where spirits pray.

Death! The Beethoven of Bereavement,
composing loss in minor tones.
You are the glorious Gaudí of Goodbyes,
revealing what the living disown.

The McGregor of Moves and Mantra,
You crooned Zion through sorrow's release.
Ah, Lady Hall of Harvest and Hosannas,
You sang: "Before the burial comes the feast."

O Coverley, chronicler of Customs in Creole,
voicing last rites in bush-wisdom and will.
Queen of the Maroons, Mystic of Midnight,
at Your call, the very air stood still.

The Desmond of Dignified Dissent,
You mark the place where tyranny ends.
Death, the King of Kin and Cry,
drum major of the marches the bereaved attend.

IX. *Invitation*

Who is Death in your litany?
A child? A migrant? A daring sight?
This poem has just begun. Its verses await
the names who keep you up at night.

X. *Benediction*

And so, this beautiful thing called Death,
You came once more to take, curse, and bless,
not in silence, but in syllables of last breath.
O, how I ache for You, my Aphadonis.

Part

II.

Companion
Resource

Facilitator's Companion for Death:
The Epithet of Excellence

This section provides support for educators, retreat leaders, and facilitators using this work in communal, liturgical, or classroom settings. It includes writing prompts, ritual suggestions, performance tips, and contextual reflections for engaging with each part of the poem.

I. Prologue: Naming the Guest

    a. Begin with silence or a centering breath.

    b. Invite participants to reflect on how they have imagined or feared Death.

    c. Prompt: *"If Death knocked on your door, what name would you give it?"*

II. The Artists of Loss

    a. Project images of Michelangelo's *Pietà* or Picasso's *Guernica*.

    b. Discuss how art can carry collective or ancestral grief.

    c. Prompt: *"What do you create when you grieve?"*

III. The Sound of Departure

    a. Play a short clip of a classical piece (e.g., Rachmaninoff's *Prelude in C# Minor*).

    b. Invite participants to journal on sounds that linger after a loss.

    c. Prompt: *"What note or silence marked your goodbye?"*

IV. Vision and Dream

   a. Share surreal or symbolic art (Van Gogh, Escher, Dalí).

   b. Discuss how dreams hold memory and loss.

   c. Prompt: *"Have you ever dreamed of someone or something you have lost? Describe the dream and what it meant to you."*

V. The Writers of Grief

   a. Encourage sharing of personal elegies, diary entries, or obituaries.

   b. Prompt: *"What story did Death write into your life?"*

VI. The Comedy and Chaos of Dying

   a. Invite conversation about humor and irreverence in funerals, wakes, or grief.

   b. Use a video clip (e.g., George Carlin) if appropriate.

   c. Prompt: *"What made you laugh when you or others thought you shouldn't?"*

VII. Lament and Mystery

   a. Create a space for quiet, candlelight, or reflective music.

   b. Invite the use of tactile materials (fabric, herbs, or thread) to hold, weave, or arrange as a form of embodied mourning.

   c. Prompt: *"What sacred objects hold your mourning?"*

VIII. Song, Spirit, and Reckoning

   a. Use news clips, protest art, or spirituals to introduce justice-oriented grief.

   b. Prompt: *"Who taught you that grief could speak truth to power?"*

IX. Invitation

    a. Encourage participants to write their own stanzas beginning with: "Who is Death in your litany?"

    b. Optional: Create a visual wall or altar of names.

X. Benediction

    a. Read aloud by a single voice or chorus.

    b. Allow silence afterward, then invite final offerings (words, gestures, objects).

These facilitation notes are designed to deepen the poem's reach and resonance. Feel free to adapt your activities based on your group's context, time, and emotional needs.

A Note on Death and Grief

Death is not one thing. Neither is grief.

Some encounter it with discretion. Others with rage. Some rituals soothe. Others cannot find their form. Grief may arrive as silence, satire, chant, memory, numbness, or noise. It belongs to no tradition and yet lives within all of them.

This work does not attempt to define death, dying, or bereavement. Instead, it creates space for story, witness, naming, and art.

Poetry, like grief, does not resolve. It lingers. It waits. It dares to speak when language feels fragile.

If this book is anything, it is an invitation to hold death with more than despair. Hold it with reverence. With paradox. With presence.

Whatever death has meant for you, may this litany create more space.

For the Names Still Waiting...

_____

_____

_____

_____

_____

_____

_____

_____

_____

_____

_____

_____

_____

_____

_____